History's Greatest Mysteries: The Nazca Lines

By Charles River Editors

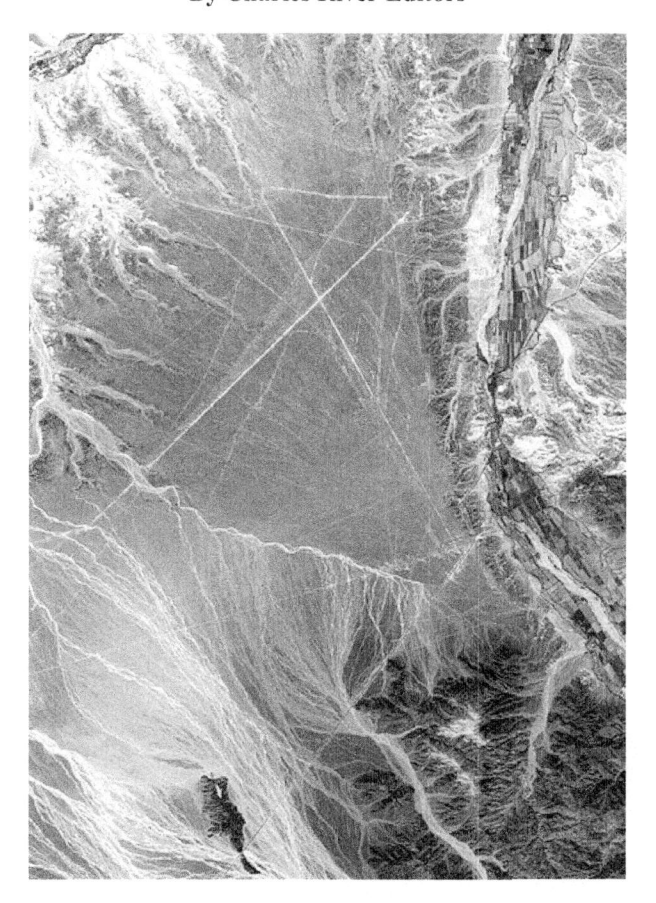

Satellite photo of Nazca Lines

About Charles River Editors

Charles River Editors was founded by Harvard and MIT alumni to provide superior editing and original writing services, with the expertise to create digital content for publishers across a vast range of subject matter. In addition to providing original digital content for third party publishers, Charles River Editors republishes civilization's greatest literary works, bringing them to a new generation via ebooks.

Introduction

Aerial photo of Nazca Lines

The Nazca Lines

"The geometric ones could indicate the flow of water or be connected to rituals to summon water. The spiders, birds, and plants could be fertility symbols. Other possible explanations include: irrigation schemes or giant astronomical calendars." – Cynthia Stokes Brown

In 1927, Today, millions of people fly, and everyone who does views the ground thousands of feet below. But in 1927, air traffic was a relatively new phenomenon, especially in the wilds of southern Peru, and when the first planes passed over the sprawling expanse of the Nazca Desert, passengers looking out their windows saw an incredible sight that they could hardly believe. On the baked desert floor, someone had carved broad, perfectly straight Lines that ran for miles. Even more amazingly, some of the Lines twisted together to form the shapes of animals, birds and insects. But when the Lines were investigated further, it was discovered that they were mostly undetectable from ground level. As researcher Viktoria Nikitzki put it, "The Lines themselves are superficial, they are only 10 to 30 cm deep."

Since their discovery, these "geoglyphs" (the name for any large carving viewable from the air)

have attracted attention from the around the world, and their popularity is matched only by the mystery surrounding them. Why were they created? Who drew the Lines? What technology did they use to fashion them? Their beauty and mystery have, at times, led to farfetched theories that have credited extraterrestrials; as one National Geographic article on the Nazca Lines put it, "At one time or another, they have been explained as Inca roads, irrigation plans, images to be appreciated from primitive hot-air balloons, and, most laughably, landing strips for alien spacecraft."

Despite elaborate modern fantasies about aliens and spaceships, the New Age theories have obscured the genius of the Lines' human creators. In fact, the creation of the Lines was actually well within the technology of the purported builders, and the Lines could be drawn without extraterrestrial excavators. Luckily, decades of dedicated archeology have begun to slowly peel back many of these mysteries, even as new discoveries have opened the door for new questions and new puzzles. To this day, anthropologists, archaeologists and other scholars continue to debate whether the Lines had religious importance, astronomical importance, or were made for entirely different reasons.

History's Greatest Mysteries: The Nazca Lines explores these amazing Lines from a number of different angles. This book looks at the physical context of the Lines (including the geology, climate, proximity to population centers, etc) and explains how the unique landscape allowed the Lines to be created in the first place and aided in their preservation over the centuries, only to be discovered anew in the 20th century. It also examines just what the Nazca Lines are, including what forms they take. This book also looks at the culture of the people who lived there, including the other archaeological remains of the Nazca people and what is known about their economy, society, and political structure. Along the way, *History's Greatest Mysteries: The Nazca Lines* comprehensively covers the facts, mysteries, and theories surrounding the phenomenon. Together with pictures and a bibliography, you will learn about the Nazca Lines like you never have before, in no time at all.

A pattern of Nazca Lines known as "The Hummingbird". Photo by Martin St-Amant

Chapter 1: The Landscape of the Nazca Desert

The Nazca Lines are fundamentally connected to their location in Sechura Desert, and thanks to the Lines, the desert is often called the Nazca Desert. The desert is located in the southern corner of Peru, and its climate, geology, topography and isolation were all critical to both the creation and the preservation of these geoglyphs into the modern age. Thus, any understanding of the Lines must start with the desert landscape itself.

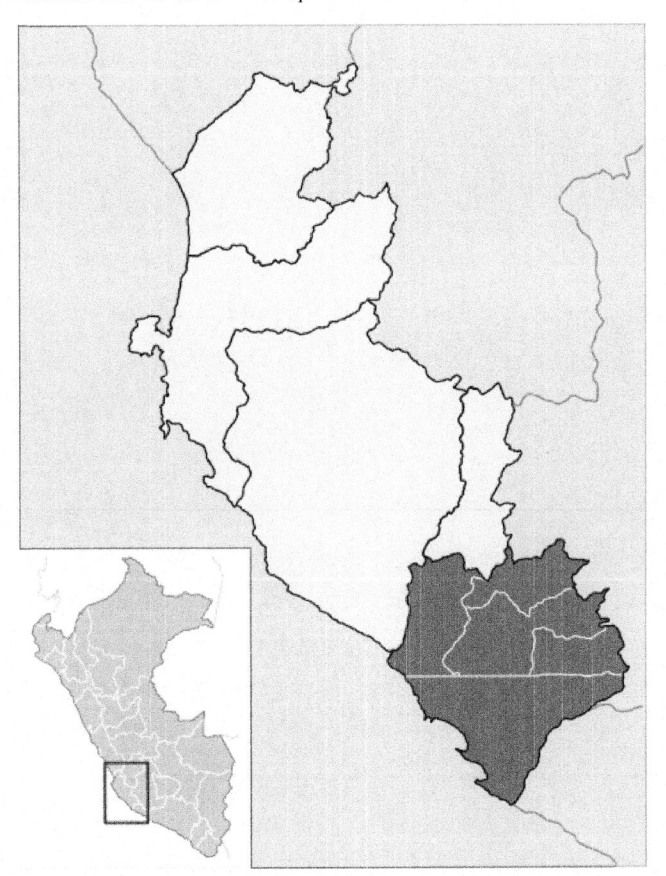

The location of the desert in Peru is highlighted

Peru's geography, like that of the entire Andean region, is defined by several distinct climate zones. Although the Pacific Ocean is directly west of the coastal deserts there, the deserts are some of the driest places on Earth, such as the famous Atacama Desert which stretches along much of Peru's coastline. Moving east from the deserts, the foothills of the Andes begin to rise up, leading quickly to the Andean highlands. After crossing the cordilleras (mountain ranges) of the Andes, the eastern side of the mountains brings travelers to a landscape that is a stark opposite to the western deserts: the lush rainforests of the Amazon Basin[1].

The lives of the peoples of ancient, Pre-Columbian Peru - as well as of modern Peruvians - are defined in large part by these regions; to this very day, almost all coastal settlements are concentrated along river valleys and their harbors. For example, the modern metropolis of Lima, home to 9 million people, is located in the valleys of the Lurín, Chillón and Rímac rivers. Closer to the Nazca Lines, the city of Tumbes is in the valley of the Tumbes River, and the city of Piura (just north of the Sechura Desert) is located along the banks of the river of the same name. The ancient creators of the Nazca Lines almost certainly lived in a similar environment, likely drawing water from the rivers to irrigate their fields and allow them to build their cities in a land without rain. This means that even within the relatively limited zone of desert terrain that the Nazcans controlled, there were two distinct zones. The valley lowlands had access to water, were fertile and supported all of their agriculture and their cities. In contrast, the plateaus surrounding the valleys were virtually unpopulated and completely without surface water sources.

However, it was not the densely populated valleys where they chose to create their geoglyphs but rather the waterless deserts of the upland plateaus. The Sechura Desert is relatively narrow, hugging the coast, and its dryness cannot be over-emphasized; in some areas of the Peruvian coastline, there is no trace (neither in the written record nor in the geological one) of there ever having been rainfall. The cause of this unique situation is that the weather in the area is dominated by the "Humboldt Current," which draws up seawater and air from Antarctica, the driest of continents and one that has almost no surface water itself. This means that delicate features on the landscape, including the famous geoglyphs, do not wash away over the centuries and are only subject to weathering from the wind[2].

Geologically, the region is characterized by volcanic stones overlaid by a layer of sand and coarse rock. The rocks of the area are the relatively recent product of tectonic action and a layer of organic matter (necessary for true soil) that has not developed because of the scarceness of plant life. In some areas, the sandy layer is so thin that all of the sand can be easily scraped off with tools, exposing the bedrock below.

Peru is a vast country, but because the population centers are concentrated in its coastal valleys (especially around Lima, far to the south of the Sechura) and in the highlands around the ancient capital of Cuzco, much of its interior is sparsely populated and rarely visited. The Sechura

---

1 "Peru: Vegetation" and "Peru: Population" (1970) map found at the Perry-Castañeda Library of the University of Texas online map collection. Accessed online at: http://www.lib.utexas.edu/maps/peru.html.
2 "Sechura Desert" (2008) in the *Encyclopedia of the Earth*, Mark McGinley (ed.) accessed online at: http://www.eoearth.org/view/article/155957/

Desert is just such a place, and it is probable that the ancient Nazcans chose it as the location of their Lines because it far enough removed from the landscape of their everyday activities. With no reason to farm, settle or even visit amongst the Lines, they were left relatively untouched until the 20th century. In this way, the landscape of the Sechura Desert served not only as the perfect canvas for the Nazcans' greatest art but also served as the art's greatest protector for centuries. As discussed further below, this natural protection has only begun to break down in the 20th century as the population finally began to spill out of the valleys and up into the highlands.

Despite this fortuitous location, the Lines' isolation was probably not planned as such by the builders. Recent archaeology has shown that the region was probably not as inhospitable for the ancient Nazcans as it is today. At the same time, it appears that the Nazcans completely deforested their valley and left the ecology of the region unable to handle disastrous floods that occurred around 500 A.D. and flooded the Nazcan city of Ica.[3] The Nazca declined precipitously, and after their decline the region never recovered its vibrancy as a center of civilization. This meant fewer people, but it also ensured less wear and tear on the Lines until the present day.

Chapter 2: A Description of the "Lines"

In 1998, Robert McG. Thomas Jr. wrote about the Lines in the *New York Times* and described them for readers:

> "To see the Lines near Nazca, in southern Peru, from the air - and there is no other way to make out the fabulous figures, some hundreds of yards across - the vast tapestry looks very much like the haphazard markings on a giant child's chalkboard.
>
> There is a monkey with a whimsical spiral tail here, a condor there -- a whale, a shark, a pelican, a spider, a hummingbird, an owl-faced man, a pair of hands, other birds and animals, flowers, and an array of geometric shapes. There is also a profusion of string-straight Lines, some extending for miles, none suggesting an immediate explanation of why they were drawn."[4]

---

3 "Peru's Nazca Culture was Brought Down with its Trees" (2009) by Thomas H. Maugh II in *The Los Angeles Times* accessed online at: http://www.latimes.com/news/nationworld/nation/la-sci-nazca2-2009nov02,0,2088132.story

4 "Maria Reiche, 95, Keeper of an Ancient Peruvian Puzzle, Dies" (1998) by Robert McG Thomas Jr. in *The New York Times* accessed online at: http://www.nytimes.com/1998/06/15/world/maria-reiche-95-keeper-of-an-ancient-peruvian-puzzle-dies.html?pagewanted=all

Nazca Lines depicting a Pelican

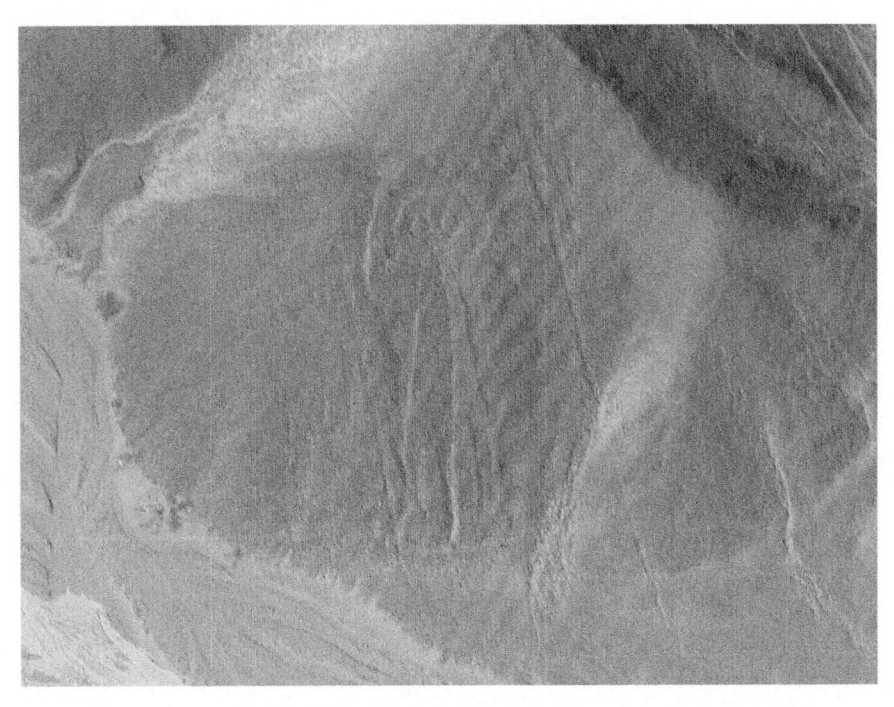

Nazca Lines that seemingly depict a human with an owl's face, also known as the Giant

Nazca Lines depicting a Spider

There are two main ways that the geoglyphs can be categorized: by time period and by style. For their part, archaeologists and art historians have divided the creation of the Lines into three periods, and at least at first glance, time period seems to be the most straightforward method for categorizing art. After all, Western art historians constantly discuss art in the context of time periods, evolution of styles and the ways that predecessors influenced the art that came after them, such as the way the Renaissance influenced the subsequent Impressionists.

However, the main problem with this approach is that the ancient Nazcans did not possess writing[5], so it's extremely difficult to date any type of stone construction simply based upon analysis of the materials. Whether a Nazca line was carved a thousand years ago or four hundred years ago is difficult to determine, and this has stymied a lot of traditional analysis.

Of course, these are problems that archaeologists face not just the Sechura Desert but across the world, so they have endeavored to find ways around the problem. There are two ways archaeologists date buildings and objects: relative and absolute dating. Absolute dating is the use of primarily chemical analysis techniques to determine exactly when an event (such as the creation of an object) occurred. The most famous example is "Carbon 14," a mildly radioactive

---

5 Nor did any South American people, though the Incas possessed a form of numeric record-keeping that involved knotted ropes called "quipus," they could not be used to tell stories.

element that builds up in living beings and then begins to decay radioactively after their death. The fact that this decay occurs at a fixed rate allows archaeologists to give an exact number of years since the death of a creature.[6] However, the creation of the Lines did not involve killing any living things - there are no bones or wood fragments present - and other absolute techniques also fail to produce information. Instead, archaeologists must use the other form of dating: relative dating. In relative dating techniques, an archaeological item or feature is compared to other similar objects, and those with a similar style are put in groups. Then the archaeologist finds intermediate forms and can subsequently attempt to create a timeline of changes. For example, classical archaeology often focused on the analysis of ceramic forms; once a timeline of ceramics was created, the archaeologist was able to place not only any ceramic piece found in that timeline but also any other objects found alongside those ceramics.

This painstaking process has allowed for modern archaeologists to understand at least some basic information about the histories of peoples without written records, like the Nazcans. In the case of the Nazca Lines, art historians have worked to date the Lines by doing a sophisticated analysis of the styles and comparing them to artistic motifs found in other types of art, such as textiles and ceramics. These other art forms are more amenable to both absolute dating (especially textiles) and relative dating, and they are associated with the everyday places that made up the majority of the Nazcan lives.

Through this elaborate system, scholars have determined that the Lines were created in three distinctive phases. The first period dated from roughly 500-300 B.C., and in this period the geoglyphs were created by piling stones in shapes. This period roughly corresponds with a time when the Andean coast was dominated by the Chavín Empire to the south of Nazca. The second phase ran from 400-200 B.C. and was associated with the creation of the local Paracas culture, which is discussed further below. In this period, the Lines were created by piling rocks into shapes on hillsides which could be seen from the desert floor. The final period, lasting from 200 B.C. to 500 A.D., is the "Nazca" period, and the majority of the geoglyphs date from that period.[7] These Lines were typically made on the floor of the desert. After this period, however, the Line-making tradition appears to have disappeared quickly. By the time the Spanish (and their chroniclers) conquered Peru in the 1530s, a thousand years had passed and none of the local natives had any memory of the Lines.

The second way of categorizing the Lines is by style. This differs from the previous form of categorization because different styles were created during the same time period, especially during the final "Nazca" stage. The existence of different styles coexisting in the same time period is similar to Modern Art, where various motifs and styles are used - sometimes by a single artist - during the same time period. Amongst the surviving Nazca Lines, the two most important styles are the "biomorph" images and the straight Lines.

---

6 "Carbon-14 Dating" accessed online at: http://www.chem.uwec.edu/Chem115_F00/nelsolar/chem.htm
7 "Nazca Lines UNESCO World Heritage Service Advisory Body Evaluation" (1994)

The "biomorph" images are easily the most photogenic of the Lines. They are shapes carved into the desert in forms of animals, plants and geometric designs. A list of images includes: the Orca/Shark, the Shells, the Frigate Bird, the Flamingo, the Parrot, the Spiral, the Sea Plant, the Hands, the Mushroom, the Fan/Star, the Top Spiral, the Llamas, the Dog, the Monkey, the Hummingbird, the Spider, the Condor and the Baby Condor and the Tree[8]. Despite that lengthy list, this is probably not complete, as new images are still discovered on occasion and it's possible that some have been destroyed over the centuries.

The Condor. Photo by Raymond Ostertag

---

8 "Nazca Lines - Google Earth" at Aquiziam World Mysteries, accessed online at:
http://www.aquiziam.com/nazca-Lines-google-earth.html

The Dog

The Hands

The Frigate Bird

Nazca Lines depicting a bird that looks like a heron. Photo by Marcito

The majority of these images were formed by a single twisting line which forms the image, but there are a number that were created by scraping away the earth inside the image, creating an appearance of negative space on the desert surface. While the image formed using this technique lacks much in the way of detail and is more like a stylized silhouette, they are still usually very obvious in what form they take. For example, the Monkey is instantly identifiable, and the Hummingbird delights visitors with the clarity of its wings and feathers. That said, a few continue to elicit debate, such as the one that might be a fan or a star. Another one might be an orca or shark. But these are the exceptions, not the rule.

In addition to those images, the more common, and possibly more impressive, Lines are the ones in geometric shapes. Some of the Lines run for tens of miles, and yet they are broad and straight as they run across the desert plateau.[9] In addition to these famous straight Lines, they also take a number of shapes, especially trapezoids and areas of cleared ground in rectangular shapes, as well as collections of rays and spirals[10].

---

9 "Spirits in the Sand: The Ancient Nasca Lines of Peru Shed Their Secrets" by Stephen S. Hall (2010) at *National Geographic Online*, accessed online at: http://ngm.nationalgeographic.com/2010/03/nasca/hall-text
10 "New Evidence for the Date of the Nazca Lines" (1991) by Helaine Silverman and David Browne, published in the journal *Antiquity* v. 65 no. 221 pp. 208-220, accessed online at:

Satellite image of lines

Even today, researchers are amazed by how remarkably straight the straight Lines are. Moreover, they do not vary with the terrain, as if they were drawn with a straight edge ruler across the landscape. While not nearly as photogenic as the images of various animals, it is these Lines that have ignited much of the debate and speculation over the Lines and their purpose. Why would anyone draw a giant line across the desert? It has no immediately apparent beauty, and any conceivable purpose is frustratingly enigmatic. These questions, and the various theories proposed to answer them, are the topic of a subsequent chapter.

---

http://www.antiquity.ac.uk/Ant/065/Ant0650208.htm

Aerial photo of straight Lines

Another useful way to understand the Nazca Lines is to compare them to other geoglyphs found around the globe. While the Nazca Lines are perhaps the most famous of their type, geoglyphs were actually a relatively common form of art in the Pre-Columbian Andes. A few of the more prominent examples include the Purús geometric earthworks of eastern Peru[11], the Sajama Lines of Bolivia, the Paracas Candelabra of Peru, the Atacama Giant and numerous recent discoveries in the Amazon[12]. For example, like many of the Nazca Lines, the Sajama Lines are stunningly straight and cover tens of miles; researchers at the University of Pennsylvania noted, "While many of these sacred lines extend as far as ten or twenty kilometers (and perhaps further), they all seem to maintain a remarkable straightness despite rugged topography and natural obstacles. The sheer number and length of these lines is often difficult to perceive from ground level, but from the air or hilltop vantage points, they are stunning."

---

11 "Pre-Columbian geometric earthworks in the upper Purús: a complex society in western Amazonia" (2009) by Martti Pärssinen, Denise Schaan and Alceu Ranzi in the journal *Antiquity*, accessed online at: http://antiquity.ac.uk/ant/083/ant0831084.htm
12 "Once Hidden by Forest, Carvings in Land Attest to Amazon's Lost World" (2012) by Simon Romero in *The New York Times* http://www.nytimes.com/2012/01/15/world/americas/land-carvings-attest-to-amazons-lost-world.html?_r=2&

The Paracas Candelabra. Photo by Bruno Girin

Beyond Latin America, there are a number of other geoglyphs in scattered areas of the world, including the prominent chalk carvings of southwest England, the Maree Man of Australia (which is a relatively recent construction)[13], and the "Works of the Old Men" of Arabia.[14][15] Perhaps the most famous non-Andean geoglyphs are the English chalk carvings. These are images that were fashioned by cutting away the green turf from the white stone below, such as the Cerne Abbas Giant, the Uffington White Horse and the Long Man of Wilmington. The English images differ from the Nazca Lines primarily in that they have never been forgotten and have always existed in the public eye. In fact, they need to be regularly maintained by removing newly grown turf from the Lines, whereas the Nazca Lines were lost but survived centuries without maintenance.

---

13 "Top Ten Geoglyphs: UK & the World", accessed online at: http://www.britainexplorer.com/top-ten-geoglyphs.html
14 "Visible Only From Above, Mystifying 'Nazca Lines' Discovered in Mideast" by Owen Jarus for NBC News http://www.nbcnews.com/id/44531708/ns/technology_and_science-science/#.UfcyMm1t5RJ
15 "The 'Works of the Old Men' in Arabia: remote sensing in interior Arabia" (2011) by David Kennedy in *The Journal of Archaeological Science*, v. 38 ,i. 12, pp. 3185-3203. Accessed online at: http://www.sciencedirect.com/science/article/pii/S0305440311001907

Chapter 3: Making the Nazca Lines

Despite the mystery and often supernatural theories that have long been associated with them, the Nazca Lines were created using a remarkably simple process that relied on the distinctive geology of the Sechura Desert. In the broad plateaus where the Lines were created, the land is composed of hard, light volcanic rocks covered with a dark, sandy surface layer. The creation of small Lines was relatively simple; workers with hand tools scraped away the surface rocks and left behind a mark. This technique did not require laborers to be specialists, but it did require a large amount of labor. Even if the work was stretched out over centuries, it still required entire communities to work together. The laborers needed to have food and water brought up into the work places and needed to coordinate their work so that they could consult with the Lines' designers.

Beyond the work in the deserts, there must have been a considerable amount of planning beforehand as well, including surveying potential sites, agreeing upon the designs, setting of dates, and coordinating the various work teams. All of this implies a high degree of centralization and coordination between communities, though perhaps not to the level of a centralized state like the later Incan and Spanish Empires. There are examples of non-state peoples achieving similarly impressive results in other areas of the world without needing an overarching government demanding their labor, and the use of slaves for manual labor was a norm for thousands of years, but there is no evidence of forced labor amongst the Nazcans, and the same goes for Stonehenge in southern England and the various mounds built in North America by the Mississippian Native Americans. All of these examples indicate that people can create incredible monuments voluntarily.

Naturally, the layout of the larger patterns would have required greater specialization than the actual physical construction of the Lines, and experimental archaeologists have attempted to reconstruct the Lines with the technology available to the ancient Nazcans to test how the people might have made the lines. Maria Reiche, a German archaeologist who became one of the most devoted researchers and protectors of the Nazca Lines in the 20th century, developed one of the most plausible theories. First, she speculated that Lines were created on a small scale on two meter plots of desert (some of which are still visible alongside the final Lines). The model was broken into parts: straight Lines were created by cords suspended between wooden stakes and curves by attaching a similar cord to a single stake and drawing out the arc. In this way, Reiche demonstrated how even the most complex Lines could be broken down into a collection of straight and curved Lines, and she even found evidence of the locations of the holes that might have been created by the posts. The Nazcans' familiarity with plotting designs on grids, a skill that is fundamental to the art of weaving on a loom and was known throughout the Andes, would certainly have assisted in the planning. After analyzing countless Lines, Reiche concluded the Nazcans had a basic unit of measurement equal to 32.2 centimeters (12.68 inches), and that all of the Lines utilize this measurement. These techniques may have first been perfected by the Paracas people, the Nazcans' predecessors, who built their Lines on hillsides and were therefore able to view the final product[16].

Maria Reiche

Chapter 4: The Nazca Culture

The most plausible creators of the Lines are the culture known as the Nazca,[17] a relatively long-lasting political and ethnic group that emerged in the 2nd century B.C. and lasted nine centuries until being replaced (perhaps conquered or driven out) by the Wari in the 7th century. The Wari were one of the most powerful groups in the pre-Incan Andes and were eventually conquered by the emerging Incan Empire[18]. Dating the Nazca - and hence, their Lines - has been a complex subject for several decades, but attempts have been helped recently through the use of sophisticated absolute dating techniques. Recent scholarship has placed the flourishing of Nazca culture at between 200 and 600 A.D., with the population located primarily in the Ica river valley to the north of the Lines.[19]

The name "Nazca", which is used for the Lines, the ancient culture, and even the entire southernmost province of Peru and a nearby city, is probably a Pre-Columbian name and seems to have originally been given to the city.[20] However, it is probable that the ancient people did

---

16 "The Nazca Lines Revisited: Creation of a full size duplicate" by Joe Nickell, for *Skeptical Inquirer* (1983), accessed online at: http://www.onagocag.com/nazca.html
17 "Nazca" and almost all pre-Incan Andean names are either modern inventions or borrowed from much later peoples. It is probable the Nazca did not call themselves by that name, but we will never know their own names.
18 "Nazca Culture." (2005). In *Cassell's Peoples, Nations and Cultures*. Accessed online at: http://www.credoreference.com.libezproxy2.syr.edu/entry/orionpnc/nazca_culture
19 "New Evidence for the Date of the Nazca Lines" (1991) by Helaine Silverman and David Browne, published in the journal *Antiquity* v. 65 no. 247 pp. 208-220, accessed online at: http://www.antiquity.ac.uk/Ant/065/Ant0650208.htm
20 "Nazca" in the *American Heritage Dictionary*, accessed online at http://www.yourdictionary.com/nazca

not carry this name or call themselves by it. It is a common archaeological practice to name ancient finds after the place of their discovery (for example the Neanderthals are named after Germany's Neandertal River, and the Mississippian Mound Builders got their name from their region). Due to the lack of writing in the Pre-Columbian Andes and the massive cultural destruction caused by the Spanish conquest, researchers will likely never be able to determine what these people called themselves.

The predecessors of the Nazca were a people who are today called the "Paracas", a group that lived in the same region and were probably the ancestors of the Nazca[21]. Both the Paracas and the Nazca were agriculturalists but heavily supplemented their diets with hunting and gathering wild plants. The Pre-Columbian Andes were a region with a wide variety of local domesticated plants, including potatoes, beans, manioc, quinoa, chenopodium, sweet potatoes, chilis, and coca. They also raised crops that arrived from other areas of the Americas, like corn, squash, peanuts, and tapioca[22]. However, they only had a few domesticated animals: guinea pigs, muscovy ducks,[23] llamas, and vicuñas (the llamas' cousins). Many of these plants and animals thrived in the high altitudes far away from the arid valleys of the Nazca. This meant that even before the emergence of large empires like the Wari, Tiwanaku and Inca, there was a widespread network of trade threading through the coast, the highlands and the distant jungles that connected the peoples of western South America. The Lines themselves reflect these connections; the Monkey showed intimate knowledge of jungle species, and the Orca/Shark links to the downriver maritime trade.

The relative paucity of nearby sources of domesticated protein (neither the ducks nor the guinea pigs are large animals and the llamas did not live locally) meant that the Nazca never would have abandoned hunting as an important food source. It was probably hunting that drew them up out of the valleys and into the surrounding desert plateaus, the location where they would produce their incredible Lines. Thus, it would be incorrect to think of the Nazca as an isolated people. The Nazca were focused in the valleys, but they also integrated all of the surrounding areas into their economic and social systems.

In addition to their famous line drawings, the Nazca were known for their textiles and pottery art. These items are not only interesting in their own right, they have also been important to the study of the Lines, as art historians have used them for comparison in attempting to discover when particular artistic styles appeared amongst the Nazca. Traditionally, archaeologists use the development of "slip" pottery to mark the beginning of the Nazca era (as opposed to the Paracas period before it). Slip pottery is a term used to describe a ceramic technology where a layer of clay and other minerals was applied to rough pot and then it was fired, creating a smooth surface.

---

21 "Paracas." (2005). In *The Crystal Reference Encyclopedia*. Accessed online at: http://www.credoreference.com.libezproxy2.syr.edu/entry/cre/paracas
22 "Plant Domestication: Table of Dates and Places" by K. Kris Hirst, accessed online at: http://archaeology.about.com/od/domestications/a/plant_domestic.htm
23 "Muscovy Ducks: An Unusual Bird to Go with an Unusual Face", accessed online at: http://voices.yahoo.com/muscovy-ducks-unusual-bird-go-unusual-1535339.html

While elaborately decorated textiles were common amongst the Paracas people, during the Nazca period, this emphasis slowly shifted until ceramics became the dominant art form.

The Nazcans were part of a larger universe of Andean art, which tended to emphasize symmetry and stark contrasts between light and dark or positive and negative images. This focus is readily apparent in the Lines. With their contrasting simplicity between the light color of the line and the darkness of the surrounding soil, the Lines are a classic example of this type of artistic sensitivity. The Nazcans took the Paracas styles and went in their own unique direction, incorporating more sophisticated technology, larger labor parties and more elaborate rituals[24].

Anthropologists think the ancient Nazcans did not have a single central government but a society organized around local centers of power called "chiefdoms." A classic chiefdom does not have a standing military or a bureaucracy, and it is controlled by a leader who has risen to power through cunning or strength of arms to dominate a region. Upon this leader's death, the government tends to collapse, and nearby up-and-coming chiefs absorb its population through conquest. It is probable that the frontiers of the Nazca chiefdoms were set by the natural boundaries of the desert plateaus, and each one likely controlled a river valley or several small valleys. With that said, the separate chiefdoms does not necessarily mean that the Nazcans didn't view themselves as belonging to the same culture. Ancient history is full of examples in which a group of people shared a language, culture and sense of identity without having a single government, most notably the Ancient Greeks. The same could also be said of the medieval Italians, and even the modern Germans.[25]

The Nazcans appeared to be just such a people, and one of the cultural elements that they held in common was a religious system which they depicted in their art, including their Lines. They also apparently gathered at a site called Cahuachi, which was once thought to be a "capital" but is now believed to be a ritual center, the way Mount Olympus was for the Ancient Greeks: it periodically served as a site for important rituals and was seen as belonging to all of the Nazcans, but it had no political authority over them. It was outside of the biggest population centers of the Ica Valleys and located near the famous Lines themselves.

The ancient Nazcans appeared to have a relatively egalitarian society, which archaeologists have surmised by examining their burials. When a society is stratified into distinct social classes, there are typically different graves for lower class and upper class individuals, and the differences are usually quite conspicuous. However, in societies like the Nazcans', there are differences in graves but no sharp divides into groups. Instead, the differences are usually noted by a spectrum of surviving grave-goods, the items a deceased person was buried with. This is

---

24 *Art of the Andes: From Chavin to Inca* by Rebecca Stone Miller (1995). London: Thames and Hudson. Pp 66 - 82
25 We tend to think of the Germans as those who live in Germany, but "German-ness" in the Twentieth century has included people from modern Germany, East and West Germany (both 1949-1990), Austria, Switzerland, eastern France, Luxembourg, Liechtenstein, the Free City of Danzig (1920-1939) and Occupied Berlin (1945-1990).

among the most important evidence that the Nazca Lines were not created by slaves or any other model of forced labor, and unlike the Egyptian pharaohs, the Nazcans did not have an all-powerful king who could control an army of slaves and creates a monument to his glory. In situations where people are relatively equal in their wealth and status, monuments like the Lines that require vast amounts of labor must be the product of some amount of desire amongst the builders.[26]

Chapter 5: Theories about the Lines' Purpose

Perhaps the biggest reason people have been fascinated by the Nazca Lines since their rediscovery is the fact that the purpose for drawing the lines remains unknown. After all, people without the technology of flight constructed giant images that were only truly visible from the air, which has completely baffled everyone familiar with the Lines.

Of course, that has allowed for a never-ending amount of speculation, and the mystery has been a boon to the site in the years since, as it has drawn attention by researchers from around the world. The first theories held that the Lines, in particular the straight Lines, were part of a great celestial observatory. Early archaeologist Maria Reiche was an ardent proponent of this theory, and she made the first scientific maps of the site in order to demonstrate relationships between the long Lines and the trajectories of various celestial objects. However, more sophisticated archaeoastronomers, who study the connections between ancient sites like Stonehenge and celestial phenomena, have shown that there appears to be no significant connection between the Lines and events like eclipses or solstices[27].

Some theories can also be dismissed relatively easily. The theory that the Lines were roads does not seem to hold water simply because they do not seem to connect anything and often end abruptly. Likewise, the theory that they were tracks for running races does not account for the thousands of miles of distance that they cumulatively stretch. A fascinating theory which has attracted dedicated followers but not much academic enthusiasm is that the Nazcan priests built hot air balloons that they rode over the Sechura Desert. The proposer of this theory, Jim Woodman and his colleague Julian Nott, went so far as to build a hot air balloon using only technology available to the Nazcans to fly over the Lines. His remarkable creation was ultimately successful, but proving that the Nazcans could have built one is not enough to convince most archaeologists, because there is no surviving evidence that they actually did so[28]. If anything, that theory and the experimental flight were more of a testament to the way that the

---

26 "Ritual Uses of Trophy Heads in Ancient Nasca Society" by Donald A. Proulx of the University of Massachusetts from *Ritual Sacrifice in Ancient Peru*, Elizabeth Benson and Anita Cook (eds.). Austin: University of Texas Press. Pp. 119-136. 2001 Accessed online at: http://people.umass.edu/proulx/online_pubs/Ritual_Uses_of_Trophy_Heads_Texas.pdf
27 "Rituals of the Nasca Lines" (2009) by Andrew Currey. In *Archaeology* 62(3), accessed online at: http://archive.archaeology.org/0905/abstracts/nasca.html
28 "History Revisited: Julian Nott reprises his Flight Over the Plains of Nazca" by Julian Nott. Accessed online at: http://www.nott.com/Pages/Nazca_BFA-1.pdf

Lines have fired the imaginations of modern people around the globe than a plausible reconstruction of ancient life. This also stands in stark contrast to the 1983 project organized by *Skeptical Inquirer* magazine, during which enthusiasts reconstructed the "Condor Line" in a field in Kentucky using only survey technology that would have been available based off of Maria Reiche's theories of how it had been done. The full size of the "Condor Line", a 440 foot Line, was created using ground lime and survived long enough to demonstrate it would have been possible for the ancient Nazcans to have done the job.

Despite these entertaining experimental forays, a consensus has been slowly forming about the Lines among archaeologists. While not all of the questions have been answered, much has been learned in the last 80 years about the builders and their beliefs. The first element that has been agreed upon is that the site was not just for the use of the local people but was at least one part (and perhaps not even the most important part for the participants) of an important pilgrimage center. In this sense, the Lines may have been like Lourdes or Mecca for the Nazcans.[29] The Lines may have been the dramatic backdrop for visitors to the site of Cahuachi. First excavated by Italian archaeological teams in the early 1980s, they learned that Cahuachi was not a "city" in a traditional sense, as it appeared to have no military, political or mercantile districts. Instead, it appeared to have a ceremonial purpose. At its heart is the Great Temple, which was a nearly 100 feet tall pyramid, surrounded by 150 hectares (370 acres) of buildings and grounds. All of this is built upon a naturally occurring rise in the ground, giving the Great Temple a spectacular view of the surrounding countryside. The site is located at the cusp between two worlds: the confluence of two verdant river valleys and on the "pampa" - the local name for the Sechura Desert plateau containing the famous Lines[30]. Scholars believe pilgrims and priests may have ascended this spectacular pyramid and looked out over the Lines, seeing them etched upon the desert and interpreting meanings into them.

---

29 "The Archaeological Identification of an Ancient Peruvian Pilgrimage Center" (1994) by Silverman, Helaine. Published in the journal *World Archaeology* 26 (1): 1–18.
30 "The Lost City of Nasca" (1999) transcript from *Horizon* by the BBC. Accessed online at: http://www.bbc.co.uk/science/horizon/1999/nasca_script.shtml

Adobe pyramid at Cahuachi

While the excavations and discoveries at Cahuachi give some context to the Lines, they unfortunately do provide a final answer as to the Lines' purpose, at least beyond being a spectacular backdrop for rituals and ceremonies performed at the Temple. While these may have been sufficient reasons to construct the Lines, it does not appear to explain the existence of all of the Lines and thus feels insufficient for many observers.

Two theories popular amongst scholars today are that the Lines served as a spiritual labyrinth and/or possibly a map to water sources. Across the Andes, there is a tradition of walking prayers, and individuals undertaking pilgrimages (an activity performed throughout the region) will often walk towards their destinations in groups in straight Lines, intoning prayers as they passed. Archaeologist Tomasz Gorka argued that the Lines are the products (planned or unplanned) of generations of processions. An archaeologist in the team noted, "Our idea is that they weren't meant as images to be seen anymore, but stages to be walked upon, to be used for religious ceremonies." In this theory, the transfer of the Lines from being built up rock piles on hillsides to flat spaces brushed clean of rocks on the floor of the desert - a shift which characterizes the move from the Paracas to the Nazca periods - is indicative of a major change in the way that the

Lines were being used. This was also seen as accompanying a major increase in the Nazcan population, which not only provided more labor for Line construction but also put pressure upon existing ceremonial sites which may have no longer been able to handle the larger number of pilgrims[31]. In this way, they have been compared to the "labyrinths" found in some European cathedrals: winding pathways carved into the Church floor which the believer walks through while praying, uniting both bodily motion and divine prayer[32].

The other prominent theory about the use of the Lines is that they actually form a map to the locations of underground water sources.[33] It is important to note that this map would be fundamentally different from those constructed by modern cartographers; scholars of the history of maps have shown that different sets of assumptions about the world - as well as very different expectations about what maps *do* and *show* – are at the heart of pre-modern maps with non-Western contexts[34]. Maps made under completely different sets of assumptions might not look like anything that people would recognize as a map today. With this understanding, it's possible to stretch the imagination about "mapping" and envision how the Lines, pointing in specific directions with varying yet precise lengths, might have been used to indicate the sources of groundwater, a precious resource in the Sechura Desert, for the ancient Nazcans.[35]

A good comparison regarding the difference between this hypothesized map and today's maps is the difference between Western writing and the Andean quipu system. The quipus were a device used to record and remember information about countable items, such as food supplies, bolts of cloth, laborers, plantable fields, etc. They were constructed out of lengths of colored string upon which knots were made, and then the strings were collected and put onto circular rings. The position and number of knots, combined with the length and color of the string, indicated the type and number of items. In this way, the great Andean empires, especially the Inca, were able to keep track of and manage massive empires and move resources around to meet the needs of vast armies of soldiers and laborers. The quipu system performs many of the most fundamental roles of writing: it stores information, it is transportable, it can be used by individuals who did not create it, and it can be drawn upon long after it is made and the information remains unchanged. However, at the same time, it is fundamentally different than writing, since it takes a very different shape and cannot perform all of the same functions. Thus, many scholars suppose that a map made by the pre-Columbian Andeans might be similar,

---

31 "Spirits in the Sand" (2010) by Stephen S. Hall in *National Geographic Magazine*, accessed online at: http://ngm.nationalgeographic.com/2010/03/nasca/hall-text/1
32 "Nazca Lines in Peru may Have Formed a Labyrinth for Spiritual Journeys, Research Suggests" by Ryan Grenoble, published at the *Huffington Post*, accessed online at:
http://www.huffingtonpost.com/2012/12/12/nazca-Lines-labyrinth_n_2279638.html
33 "Nazca Lines May Be Giant Map of Underground Water Sources" at *Andina* accessed online at: http://www.andina.com.pe/Ingles/Noticia.aspx?id=sBGkB+rqR6M=
34 *Siam Mapped: A History of the Geo-Body of a Nation* (1994) by Thongchai Winichakul. Honolulu: University of Hawai'i Press.
35 "The Nazca Lines Project (1996 - 2000)" by Don Proulx, accessed online at:
http://people.umass.edu/~proulx/Nasca_Lines_Project.html

fulfilling functions like Western maps while taking a radically different form.

Research on both of these theories continues to this day. The supporters of the labyrinth theory study the ruins of Cahuachi and examine processions and prayer in other Andean contexts, while the supporters of the map theory scour geological surveys for the locations of subterranean aquifers and attempt to correlate them to the positions of the Lines. It is possible, of course, that the real meaning of the Lines will be found in some other theory or that it will remain lost forever, or even that both the labyrinth and map theories are simultaneously true. The nature of archaeological research, which always deals with imperfect knowledge and the partial preservation of the past, means that modern society can never be completely certain what was going on in the minds of deceased people. However, with each new excavation and every mapping project, researchers' understanding of the ancient Nazcans improves, and their ability to make informed judgments about reality of their lives increases.

Chapter 6: The Nazca Lines Today: Preservation, Tourism, Research and Speculation

"Her footsteps tell stories...The woman walks in patterns, pictures emerge in the soil... She creates her own private Nazca Lines, tattooing the Earth with her history." - Royce Vavrek, opera librettist[36]

Royce Vavrek, an opera librettist describing an upcoming opera she wrote, managed to connect the Hubble Space Telescope images to the everyday life of the characters in the work. That this author, writing a world away from the Nazca Desert in New York City and Alberta, Canada, is able to draw upon the imagery of the Nazca Lines to generate poetic meaning is telling about the ways that the Lines have come to have a life and meaning of their own in the modern world. Indeed, beginning in 1927, the Lines were catapulted from complete obscurity into an internationally renowned locale almost overnight.

The discovery of the Lines in 1927 did not lead to immediate research, mostly because the area was isolated, research funds were limited after the 1929 stock market crash, and the foreign researchers who were interested in Peru and had funding tended to be attracted by the impressive ruins of the Incan Empire found in other parts of the country, especially once Hiram Bingham brought the ruins of Machu Picchu to the world stage in 1911. While Peruvians were interested in their past, archaeological sites had not yet taken center-stage in the national identity, and there was not yet a cadre of Peruvian-born archaeologists either. On top of all that, archaeology as a discipline was still in its infancy, so there were few archaeologists around the globe at the time.

As it turned out, Peruvians could take pride in the fact that the first archaeologist to examine the site was one of their countrymen: Toribio Mejía Xesspe. Mejía examined what he thought were canals from the vantage point of the hillsides of the Sechura pampa in 1926, the year before

---

36 "The 'Hubble Cantata'" (2013) by Mario Livio in the *Huffington Post* accessed online at: http://www.huffingtonpost.com/mario-livio/the-hubble-cantata_b_3639350.html

the stunning Lines were seen from the air, but he was unable to do a detailed study at the time. Mejía would later revise his theories with the new data to state that he believed they were ceremonial roads, making him the father of the Nazca labyrinth interpretation. His observations were also important because they led American historical geographer Paul Kosok to the site. Kosok began to grasp the enormity of the site, and after he observed the sun almost setting over a line during the June solstice, he declared them to be the "Largest Astronomy Book in the World."[37]

Like Mejía, Kosok is perhaps most important for helping to pass the torch to the most important defender and researcher of the Lines. The first person to do a dedicated study of the Lines was Maria Reiche, a German woman with a mathematics background who was also a tutor to the children of her nation's diplomatic staff during the 1930s (she left Dresden in 1932) and World War II. Reiche saw the Lines in 1941 and was so fascinated that she would eventually make them her life's work, dedicating five decades to their study. Reiche built upon Kosok's work and argued for their connection to the heavens until her death, even going so far as to map all of the Lines known at the time and mark their connections to celestial events. Furthermore, she cleaned a number of them off, removing sand that had blown onto them over the centuries, and even hired guards to protect them from damage. Ms. Reiche became a Peruvian citizen in 1994, four years before her death.[38]

Since Reiche's death, her theories regarding the connections between the Lines and the visible constellations have been proven unfounded, though her protégé, an astronomer from Chicago's Adler Planetarium named Phyllis B. Pitluga, continues to argue that there is a connection. Pitluga still maintains that the Lines don't map the visible sky but actually depict the dark spaces between the stars. The theory, while impressive for its creativity, has not found much traction among her professional colleagues, who have mostly moved on to other theories. For example, Dr. Anthony F. Aveni explained, "I really had trouble finding good evidence to back up what she contended. Pitluga never laid out the criteria for selecting the lines she chose to measure, nor did she pay much attention to the archaeological data Clarkson and Silverman had unearthed. Her case did little justice to other information about the coastal cultures, save applying, with subtle contortions, Urton's representations of constellations from the highlands. As historian Jacquetta Hawkes might ask: was she getting the pampa she desired?"

Reiche was only the most dedicated of a long line of scholars that have worked on the Lines in the decades since the 1940s. This scholarship continues apace today, and it has advanced recently due to the development of ground penetrating radar, which allows for the detection of Lines that have become completely obscured to the eye and observers working with photos taken

---

[37] Quoted in: "New Evidence for the Date of the Nazca Lines" (1991) by Helaine Silverman and David Browne, published in the journal *Antiquity* v. 65 no. 247 pp. 209, accessed online at: http://www.antiquity.ac.uk/Ant/065/Ant0650208.htm

[38] "Maria Reiche, 95, Keeper of an Ancient Peruvian Puzzle, Dies" (1998) by Robert McG Thomas Jr. in *The New York Times* accessed online at: http://www.nytimes.com/1998/06/15/world/maria-reiche-95-keeper-of-an-ancient-peruvian-puzzle-dies.html?pagewanted=all

from planes by blowing sand. Researchers from Japan[39] have been particularly important in recent years, with Professor Masato Sakai of Yamagata University opening a massive center of study in 2012.[40] This followed the discovery of several new Lines in 2011 by the same team using satellite images.[41]

Global recognition of the site's unique status has also slowly grown since the time of Kosok and Reiche. The most important recognition has been the Lines' addition to the United Nations Economic, Scientific and Cultural Organization's (UNESCO) list of World Heritage sites in 1994. This list is the most prestigious global compilation of natural and cultural sites of beauty and cultural importance, and the Nazca Lines share this honor with only a handful of other Peruvian sites, including the ruins of the cities of Chan Chan, Chavín, Machu Picchu, and Caral-Supe, the historic districts of the modern cities of Cuzco, Lima and Arequipa, and the natural beauty of Huascarán, Manú and Rio Abiseo National Parks.[42] Internationally, it puts the Lines in the same categories as the Colosseum in Rome, the Statue of Liberty in New York and Beijing's Forbidden City.

Along with this growth in official international recognition has come an increase in tourism. In the final decades of the 20th century, the Lines became a major tourist attraction, and it has been integrated into the route of the most popular young people's suggested journeys through Peru. Many of these visitors hire small propeller planes from nearby towns and view the Lines in the way that they were first discovered.

Although the Lines are a marvel just to see, the growth in interest in the Lines is also due in no small part to a modern fascination with ancient sites viewed as "mysterious," including such diverse locales as Easter Island, Stonehenge and the Pyramids at Giza. While archaeological sites always have some mystery to them, given the incomplete records of ancient peoples, this industry has had the unfortunate effect of highlighting the mysteriousness and overlooking the actual historical work. By shrouding the Lines with further layers of enigma, these authors, tour guides and documentarians have, at times, been able to spin out wild theories about their origins.[43]

The classic example of this was the 1968 publication of *Chariots of the Gods*, a book by Erik Von Däniken. Von Däniken looked across the various mysterious sites around the globe and

---

39 This connection to Japan may appear puzzling at first glance, but Peru and Japan have a long bilateral history and Peru has a large population of Japanese descent. There are roughly 90,000 people of Japanese descent in the country (the second-largest such population in Latin America after Brazil) and elected a controversial Japanese-Peruvian president, Alberto Fujimori in 1990.
40 "University to Open Center at Nazca Lines" (2012) published in *The Japan Times*, accessed online at: http://www.japantimes.co.jp/news/2012/03/22/news/university-to-open-center-at-nazca-Lines/#.UfXUuG1t5RI
41 "Walking the Line: New Figures from Nazca, Peru" by Heraldo Fuenets, accessed online at: http://www.viewzone.com/nazcatheories.html
42 "World Heritage List Evaluation: Nasca" by the UNESCO World Heritage Site Advisory Body (1993), accessed online at: http://whc.unesco.org/archive/advisory_body_evaluation/700.pdf
43 "Publications: Nazca Lines" at the *Onward to the Past* website, accessed online at: http://geoLines.ru/eng/publications/NAZCA-LINES/

argued for a single, overarching theory: they are unexplained because they were in fact built by aliens or by humans with alien assistance. While Von Däniken's theories are a poorly constructed hodge-podge riddled with inconsistency and factual inaccuracy, they had the effect of capturing the public's imagination around the globe, not to mention making von Däniken a wealthy man.[44] One of the saddest elements of von Däniken's theory is that is rejects the genius and creativity of ancient peoples around the globe. Instead of admiring the phenomenal works of engineering, creative planning and artistic grace of prehistoric humans, von Däniken and similar conspiracy theorists instead look up to a non-existent race of visitors. In the process, the actual builders recede from the story, becoming merely the dupes and tools of the supposed true masters. While nobody is entirely certain why the ancient Nazcans built Lines that can be observed from the sky, it is clear that they were able to do it, and for that, people ought to be justifiably impressed with their masterpiece[45]. As Andean art historian Rebecca Stone-Miller notes:

> "Lack of a single explanation should not contribute to maintaining the illogical 'mystery' of the Lines... [The Lines'] dimensions are difficult to grasp conceptually and equally elusive visually; they are simply too large to be perceived by humans on the ground. The Nasca sense that a human audience is not necessarily the only or primary one comes as no surprise, given the values of Andean art as a whole. Their immensity was scaled to that of the earth itself and implies a celestial supernatural audience."[46]

Even outside of the admittedly fringe realm of extraterrestrial-related archaeology, "mysteriousness" remains a dominant trope in public discussions of the Lines. The best example of this is that in the last ten years, popular interest in the Lines has bubbled into the public consciousness in part due to a number of made-for-TV documentaries about the Lines. By and large, these documentaries use mystery as a tool to hook watchers. This can be seen in titles like "Mysterious Journeys," "Secrets of the Nazca Lines" and "Buried Secrets."[47]

Title	Description	Year
"Sacred Lines of Nazca"	Short Film	2003
"The Nazca Lines Explained"	Documentary	2005

---

44 *In Search of Ancient Astronauts* film by Harald Reinl (dir) (1973). http://www.imdb.com/title/tt0133018/
45 "Prehistoric E.T.: The Fantasy of Ancient Astronauts" in *Frauds Myths and Mysteries: Science and Pseudoscience in Archaeology 4th Edition* by Kenneth L. Feder (2002). New York: McGraw Hill. Pp 202-240
46 Quote from *Art of the Andes: From Chavin to Inca* by Rebecca Stone Miller (1995). London: Thames and Hudson. Pp 82
47 "Nasca Lines" at the *Internet Movie Database* (http://www.imdb.com/find?q=nasca+Lines&s=all)

"Secrets of the Nazca Lines"	*Digging for the Truth* television show	2005
"Nasca Lines"	*Mysterious Journeys* television show	2007
"Nasca Lines: The Buried Secrets"	TV Movie	2010

While a lot of work goes into preservation of past sites, archaeological sites share a singular fate: their destruction. This can happen in a number of ways, including the natural processes of decay, the inadvertent missteps of humans on the site, or even by the planned excavations of archaeologists themselves. But thankfully, the Nazca Lines are in a much better state than most. Decomposition has been slowed to a near standstill by the phenomenally harsh climate, humans have historically avoided the area, and the Lines are on the surface and thus need no destructive excavations in order to be studied. Moreover, because visitors fly over the site, it is unlikely to be "loved to death" by tourists, the potential fate of the other famous Peruvian archaeological destination, Machu Picchu.

Of course, this does not mean that there are no threats to the future of the site. In fact, there are two primary dangers to the site's long term future. The first threat is the incursion of humans into the area. Because of the fact that it is possible to walk across a Line and not realize that it is there, even well-meaning people could inadvertently cause damage to the Lines. This problem is exacerbated by the fact that the Lines are scattered across a vast landscape, so attempting to isolate them physically with fences or guards is an expensive proposition.[48]

In recent years, the populations of neighboring valleys have begun to increase, and this means that poor peasants have pushed further out in search of grazing lands for their pigs and places to build their homes. The hooves of large herds of domesticated animals, something unknown to the Pre-Columbian Americas, has caused extensive damage to some of the Lines, and if left unchecked, they could threaten to eventually wipe some of the Lines out of existence. One community of landless peasants was recently found to have built a community of 50 buildings alongside one of the Lines, and they may have accidentally destroyed a Nazca cemetery[49]. Lines have also been damaged by poorly planned road construction, something which could have been easily avoided by better coordination between the state's conservation and road-building departments.[50]

---

[48] Homepage of the Asociación Maria Reiche, accessed online at: http://www.maria-reiche.org/lineas/Home.html
[49] "Pigs and Squatters Threaten Peru's Nazca Lines" by Mitra Taj on Reuters, Aug 17th, 2012. Accessed online at: http://www.reuters.com/article/2012/08/17/us-peru-nazca-squatters-idUSBRE87E0R720120817
[50] "Heavy Machinery Destroys Nazca Lines" by Manuel Vigo (2013) at *Peru This Week*, accessed online at: http://www.peruthisweek.com/news-3743-peru-heavy-machinery-destroys-nazca-Lines/

Ultimately, the greatest threat to the Lines is neither the hooves of sheep nor the heavy machinery of the road crews but the accelerating changes of the planet's climate. As noted several times, the greatest protector of the Lines is the incredibly brutal aridity of the Sechura Desert. This dryness is dependent upon the existence of the Humboldt Current, bringing frigid air up the west coast of South America from Antarctica. However, the weather currents in South America, like the rest of the globe, are changing, and coastal deserts like the Atacama and Sechura have experienced unprecedented rains in recent years. In 2007, a relatively light snowfall in the Atacama quickly turned to mud in the parched soils, leading to disastrous mudslides in the Chilean town of Tocopilla. It was the first time there had been precipitation in Tocopilla in 30 years[51]. Much heavier snows happened down the coast in 2011, reflecting long-term changes in the region[52]. As Viktoria Nikitzki of the Maria Reiche Centre explained, "The Lines themselves are superficial, they are only 10 to 30 cm deep and could be washed away... Nazca has only ever received a small amount of rain. But now there are great changes to the weather all over the world. The Lines cannot resist heavy rain without being damaged."

The Sechura does not need to have disastrous or even regular rains to threaten the Lines - even occasional rains could spell the end of these archaeological remnants. Water moving across the baked landscape and creating mud would begin to blur the edges of the Lines immediately, and the resulting plant growth in an otherwise sterile territory would eventually produce roots. If plant life grows in the region, burrowing animals would arrive and continue the process of turning the soil and inadvertently eliminating the fragile Lines.

In 2012, the Lines were put on the World Monument Fund's Watch List for threatened monuments[53]. The Peruvian state, and other interested parties, including archaeologists, local tourist providers, and government officials, face increasing challenges in protecting the Lines. At the current moment, the Peruvian Ministry of Culture (with help from UNESCO) is facing these challenges by developing strategies to better mark the edges of the Lines on the ground, hopefully preventing the ever-growing number of incursions. Challenges from climate change are outside of the ability of the Peruvian state to handle alone and must be taken into the wider global struggle to contain and limit the effects of shifting weather patterns.

Bibliography

Aveni, Anthony F. (ed.) (1990). The Lines of Nazca. Philadelphia: American Philosophical Society. ISBN 0-87169-183-3

Haughton, Brian. (2007). Hidden History: Lost Civilizations, Secret Knowledge, and Ancient

---

51 "Atacama desert sees snow, rain after 30 years" August 27th, 2013. Accessed online at
http://www.solarnews.ph/news/world/2013/08/27/atacama-desert-sees-snow-rain-after-30-years#.UjM_-D_3NFs
52 "Driest place on Earth: Atacama Desert in Chile buried under feet of snow" by Ryan Maue, July 7th, 2011. Accessed online at: http://wattsupwiththat.com/2011/07/07/driest-place-on-earth-atacama-desert-in-chile-buried-under-feet-of-snow/
53 "Lines and Geoglyphs of Nasca" at the World Monument Fund Website, accessed online at:
http://www.wmf.org/project/Lines-and-geoglyphs-nasca

Mysteries. Career Press. ISBN 1-56414-897-1

Johnson, Emma. 2007. The 'Mysterious' Nazca Lines. PARA Web Bibliography B-01.

Kosok, Paul (1965). Life, Land and Water in Ancient Peru, Brooklyn: Long Island University Press.

Lambers, Karsten (2006). The Geoglyphs of Palpa, Peru: Documentation, Analysis, and Interpretation. Lindensoft Verlag, Aichwald/Germany. ISBN 3-929290-32-4

Nickell, Joe. 1983. Skeptikal Inquirer The Nazca Lines Revisited: Creation of a Full-Sized Duplicate.

Reinhard, Johan (1996) (6th ed.) The Nazca Lines: A New Perspective on their Origin and Meaning. Lima: Los Pinos. ISBN 84-89291-17-9

Sauerbier, Martin. GIS-based Management and Analysis of the Geoglyphs in the Palpa Region. ETH (2009). doi:10.3929/ethz-a-005940066.

Stierlin, Henri (1983). La Clé du Mystère. Paris: Albin Michel. ISBN 2-226-01864-6

von Däniken, Erich (2003). Arrival of the Gods: Revealing the Alien Landing Sites of Nazca. Vega, London. ISBN 1-84333-053-9; first published (1977) as Zeichen für die Ewigkeit, Bertelsmann Verlag, Munich.

Printed in Great Britain
by Amazon